My Teaching Days

My Teaching Days
and the Lessons I Learned

John Fairbrother

Ambassador International
GREENVILLE, SOUTH CAROLINA & BELFAST, NORTHERN IRELAND

www.ambassador-international.com

My Teaching Days
and the Lessons I Learned

© 2018 by John Fairbrother
All rights reserved

ISBN: 978-1-62020-617-1
eISBN: 978-1-62020-696-6

Scripture quotations taken from THE HOLY BIBLE, NEW
INTERNATIONAL VERSION®, NIV® Copyright © 1973, 1978, 1984, 2011
by Biblica, Inc.® Used by permission. All rights reserved worldwide.

Cover Design and Page Layout by Hannah Nichols
eBook Conversion by Anna Riebe Raats

AMBASSADOR INTERNATIONAL
Emerald House
411 University Ridge, Suite B14
Greenville, SC 29601, USA
www.ambassador-international.com

AMBASSADOR BOOKS
The Mount
2 Woodstock Link
Belfast, BT6 8DD, Northern Ireland, UK
www.ambassadormedia.co.uk

The colophon is a trademark of Ambassador

To my wife Frances and our sons Timothy and Andrew.

CONTENTS

MY TESTIMONY 11

LESSON 1
THE COST OF FOLLOWING JESUS 23

LESSON 2
CHANGING ATTITUDES ABOUT COMPETITION 27

LESSON 3
TANGIBLE POWER 33

LESSON 4
THE NEED FOR PRAYER 35

LESSON 5
THE MISSING KEY 39

LESSON 6
THE TRIBUNAL 41

LESSON 7

THE HUMAN HEART   47

LESSON 8

PROVIDENCE AND SOVEREIGNTY   51

LESSON 9

MINISTRY DURING CHRISTMASTIME   55

LESSON 10

A DIFFICULT YEAR   61

LESSON 11

TEACHING ABOUT SIN WITH
MATH LESSONS   65

LESSON 12

CHOOSING MY WORDS   67

LESSON 13

DECEPTION   71

LESSON 14

CONFIDENCE IN APPROACHING GOD   73

LESSON 15

COMPLETE IN JESUS   81

LESSON 16

ARROW PRAYERS   83

LESSON 17

OPENING DOORS   85

LESSON 18

WITNESSING TO FELLOW TEACHERS   91

LESSON 19

THE SINAI DESERT   95

LESSON 20

COMPETING IDEAS AND PHILOSOPHIES   99

LESSON 21

MEETING CHALLENGING BEHAVIOUR   103

MY TESTIMONY

I WAS BORN TOWARDS THE end of the Second World War in Middleton near Manchester, a town in Lancashire where there were numerous cotton mills with tall chimneys continually belching out smoke. My father and mother met while working in one of these mills. He was much older, his wife had died and my mother was single. For some reason, they never married and they lived together in the terraced house she rented. When three children arrived, me first, they were not entitled to any family allowance, nor any benefits from the state because they were never married legally. When I grew older I discussed this with my brother and sister and all of us felt that the state owed us nothing. We felt it should not have to pay for sin. So, we lived and grew up in a small two-up, two-down house with no inside toilet, no bathroom, no running hot water, and no electricity (gas lighting) till I was in my late teens.

Two minutes away from the house was a Baptist Church and we were sent to Sunday school every Sunday afternoon from an early age. My mother or some neighbour took us to morning services. My father was a smoker, a drinker and a gambler and was off to the pub on Sundays as soon as it opened. Of those Sunday mornings, I remember a young man training at a Baptist College in Manchester

12   My Teaching Days

coming for several consecutive Sundays and telling us children the story of "The Pilgrim's Progress" in serial form. We were gripped and could not wait for the next episode. What an impression he made, what seed was sown. These were the days when Sunday was different. No shops opened, no public transport ran till early afternoon. The Salvation Army band played hymns in the street on Sunday morning. I began to have some understanding of the Sabbath and when I was at college I had the privilege of hearing Professor Verna Wright speak on the benefits of a good Sabbath rest.

I was also blessed by attending a Church of England primary school with several Christian teachers, one of whom told us vivid Old Testament stories such as "The Crossing of the Red Sea" with colourful big pictures of Pharaoh's chariots being engulfed. We all loved her telling of these stories, and she was strict about good standards of work and behaviour. We all had to learn and recite the Apostles Creed and The Lord's Prayer for when the local vicar came in. These were days in the 1950s when bad behaviour was not tolerated and everyone feared the headmaster's cane. All this was good seed being sown and I firmly believe God's hand was upon me, protecting and preparing me for my eventual conversion in my mid-thirties.

I remember, too, in those Sunday School days the Sunday school anniversaries with large congregations to watch us children sing and recite Scripture. I remember the parades we had around the town with other Sunday schools with banners carried by strong men to the accompaniment of brass bands. We all met in the town central gardens to sing hymns and hear a message.

However, I stopped going to Sunday school and church when I became a teenager. I had passed an exam to attend the local grammar

MY TESTIMONY   13

school with several Christian teachers. We learned and sang hymns like "For All the Saints" and there were Bible readings and prayers in assembly. I developed a deep fear of God. He kept coming into my thoughts and every night before I went to bed I would stand at my bedroom window, look up to the stars and say The Lord's Prayer. I had a good friend just down the road with whom I used to play tennis in the summer months. He was a little older than me and he attended a Roman Catholic school and church. We had many discussions together about God. I thought I knew a lot about Him.

Towards the end of my teenage years, I decided to go back to the Baptist church across the road on Sunday evenings. Several of my old Sunday school teachers were there. A retired Baptist Minister had been employed, and though he was approaching 80 years old he preached powerfully, but I couldn't understand much of what he said. At age 21 I got a place in a Teacher Training College in Bingley, West Yorkshire. On my last Sunday before going off, I was asked to choose a hymn I would like sung at the evening service. I had no hesitation in choosing "My Song is Love Unknown." So off to college I went and in my hall of residence I formed a friendship with several young men who on Sunday evenings went to a small Church of England church on Ilkley Moor. We had many good conversations together in our rooms and I started going to the Christian Union with them.

While at college I learned that my teenage sister was having a baby after an affair with a fellow worker in the factory where she worked. The man wanted nothing to do with her after that so she brought the baby home to live with my mother. Years later I asked her what it was like, a single parent living in a small terraced house. What did the neighbours think when she took the baby out? She told me that she didn't dare go out the front door with the baby for fear of what the neighbours would think and say. She crept out the back door and avoided everyone. Such were the times. Unwanted teenage pregnancies were a rare occurrence then and people's attitudes to them were so much different. My sister later repented and was baptised as a believer. The baby she had, a little boy, is now a professor in a top London university.

Our wedding day in 1969 March.

In my second year at college in September 1966 I went with my friends again to the Christian Union. As I entered the room my eyes fell upon a beautiful young lady I had not seen before. I learned she went on Sunday to the local Methodist church so I went too just to get to know her. We continued to go to the Christian Union and most messages were comfortable, but one week we had a visit from a Baptist minister from the northeast. All through the message he spoke about "sin" and I felt very uncomfortable. I didn't understand "sin." Four years later we were married in her parent's Methodist church in Birmingham, also where I had moved to take up my first teaching post. Two of our Christian friends from college also had moved to the city and we kept up our friendship with them, till they told us they were expecting a baby. We were so filled with envy we stopped seeing them. We didn't go to church and for eight

MY TESTIMONY 15

years we went through some very difficult times in complete darkness and sin.

When I was in my early thirties I watched a TV documentary on growing food needs in Africa. A clock was ticking all the way through as if the need was urgent. My heart was troubled and I began to think about God again. I became interested in problems of world poverty and injustices. I joined organizations like Friends of The Earth and others supplying information on injustices in the world. None of these groups were Christian, but I thought the church should be informed about what I was learning and so we went back to the Methodist church where we married. My wife's parents were still there. We were welcomed and I was allowed to speak about social injustices and was even asked to speak at other Methodist churches in the circuit. One thing kept troubling my mind, however. In the church on one wall, all the way down in bold letters were The Ten Commandments. I kept looking at them and knew deep within that I had broken every one and I knew no remedy.

About this time a young man, Arnie, joined the teaching staff at the Primary School where I taught. He soon made a beeline to talk to me. He learned I went to a church as I was expressing my views about social injustice in the staff room. He had been a Christian, he told me, for two years while at Loughborough University through the witness of some Navigators, a Gospel organization. I became fascinated by him and watched him all the time, hoping

Staff photo 1970s, me on the far left, Arnie, who led me to consider Christ, 2nd from right.

16   My Teaching Days

I could find faults. He was different. He didn't gossip nor talk about people behind their backs as was common in the staff room. He was gracious, kind and joyful. He admitted he needed help in his teaching children for whom English was a second language.

He invited me to play football on Saturday mornings with some friends and university students from all over the world. I enjoyed playing football and after the game we went back to someone's house or flat for refreshments. What I didn't know at the time was that some were Christians witnessing to others. I couldn't understand why after I had been introduced to various people, when I bumped into them again later, they knew my name but I couldn't remember theirs. Later I realised why they knew my name. It was because they had mentioned my name in prayers to God so many times and they pictured my face. But I felt very uneasy when someone asked for quiet so that Bill could say a few words about how Jesus had been revealed to him. The first time it happened I wanted to run away.

We were invited to more Navigator evening events and one day my wife said to me, "These people have got something we haven't got." I agreed. Then one night we went to a special Navigator evening at which the American evangelist, Leroy Eims, was to speak. He took the first verses of Ephesians 2. I'd never heard these words before but I was cut to the heart: "You, like everyone are dead in trespasses and sins." The Apostle Paul said he once was. But then God quickened Paul and made him alive in Christ Jesus. By grace he was saved, saved from the punishment he deserved. God can do it for you. There is not one sin, no matter how terrible, He cannot forgive.

God was speaking to me. We came home and my wife retired to bed. I sat downstairs alone, but not alone. I fell to my knees and cried out to God, I told Him all the things I had tried to do to please Him: giving lots of our savings to Oxfam, making social injustices known in church, getting rid of our car and taking to bikes. He showed me the cross and said, "I have done something for you, for which you could never repay Me."

I argued, "Yes, I know about the cross but it can't be for me, it's only for those who have been to church all their lives. You don't know what I've done, I've messed it up, broken all Your commandments. I don't deserve anything."

His voice said, "It's for you." At that moment, He had me. I felt cleansed and forgiven and at peace with God. "I could die at peace tonight," I thought, and went to bed. I was sure it was the risen Lord Jesus who spoke to me. I also thought I can't possibly count all the many sins I must have committed since I was conceived—millions, billions, trillions—but I knew they were all dealt with on the cross of Christ. I was a new creation.

The next day I got up but by lunch time I felt dirty within again. "I'll never stay good," I thought. But once my Christian friends realised what God had done, they helped me. They got me and my wife into short studies on assurances, and they got me to learn Scripture by heart, such as 1 John 1:9: "If we confess our sins, he is faithful and just and will forgive us our sins and purify us from all unrighteousness." What a wonderfully pure spiritual nourishment this was. We had good group leaders who are still our friends many years later.

Soon after my conversion, my wife found she was pregnant. She went to see the doctor, an elderly lady, when she suspected. I remember well it was a warm May afternoon. I was working in the garden

Enjoying our first son.

when she returned in tears. "What's the matter?" I asked. She told me that the doctor said she was a silly girl and sent her away. But in my heart, I knew that God had blessed us and the following February a baby boy was born. The first child, Timothy, was born on a snowy day in February. My wife had some difficulty in labour. I patiently waited, growing quite tired. I was woken to see her being taken to the operating room. The doctor I spoke to told me it was going to be difficult. I remember going immediately outside into the snowy pavement and kneeling in the snow and crying to God. He did not fail to answer and when I went back in a big baby boy had been born. A few years later another little boy, Andrew, was born. Both those boys were prayed for every morning from the moment of conception that God would knit, form and shape them and have His hand upon them for eternity.

Now with two growing boys, late 1980s.

When I went back to the school after my conversion I felt a complete darkness over the place and mine was the only light. There were adventures, too—leading a Baptist church youth group, taking part in Holiday Bible Clubs and helping to lead several summer youth holidays away near Bala in Wales. These holidays were really blessed by the fact that just at the right time we had some younger men with canoeing and mountain climbing qualifications. The place where we stayed was on the side of a small lake with mountains all around.

Our boys grew up in church. We left their conversions to God, prayed for them and He spoke to them. When our older son was sixteen years old he wrote a letter, put it in an envelope addressed to me and left it in the kitchen. The next morning, I was first up and saw the letter. My first thoughts were that he had decided to leave home. I was bothered but didn't have time to open it, so put it in my cycle panier to read later. I travelled the seven miles to my place of work by bicycle each day. As I went down the road from home I stopped. "I must read that letter," I thought. I took it out of the panier, opened it and began to cry as I read, "Dad, I have some good news to tell you. I have given my life to Jesus Christ," and there was more on how God had spoken to him. Sadly, on the way home I stopped at a small shop and when I came out the bike had been stolen. Of all the things I was carrying in the paniers the letter from our son was the most valued and could never be replaced.

Eight years later our other son did the same thing, only this time there were two letters, one for my wife as well. He was then eighteen years old and quite rebellious. My wife and I had the same thoughts.

"He's leaving."

I could not believe what I read when I opened the letter. The words were almost the same as his older brother had written years earlier. It began, "Dear dad, you will be very pleased with what I have to tell you," and it continued with how God had spoken to him. I still have that letter. We saw them go through the waters of baptism and make a good confession of faith. We supported them through university and continued in prayer for them. Both gained a master in science in engineering, one in civil, the other in mechanical. We prayed they might find Christian wives and they have. We have witnessed their work for the Lord in their respective university towns.

Our ever-growing family in 2014.

Now we have been blessed with five grandchildren and many Christian brothers and sisters along the way. God has always been working for good. With all the grandchildren, we have seen the importance of praying for them from the moment we first heard the news they were expected. We believe God is always working. In John 5:17 Jesus says, "My Father is always at his work to this very day, and I too am working." The tense is past, present and future so the Father, Son and the Holy Spirit are always working. We believed He was knitting, forming and shaping those children and His hand was upon them. All five births were good births, relatively quick and one day we hope and pray they will be able to say as God said to Jeremiah: "Before I formed you in the womb I knew you, before you were born I set you apart." May the Holy Spirit speak to them.

Another interesting thing happened while I was walking down to church one Sunday morning. I caught up with a man and we got talking. When I asked what he did, he told me he was on parole from prison. He had murdered his wife. He was visiting the place where they both used to live and later was going back to Winson Green prison. I asked if I could visit him there and he gave me details. He

MY TESTIMONY   21

was interested to hear me talk about Jesus. A week later a Christian friend and I received permission to visit. We went through many security checks, quite a few barred gates till eventually the officer showed us the prisoners. There we could see them behind bars. What surprised me as we walked towards them was the number of young men all calling "Hello, sir!" Sadly, I recognised former pupils.

In later years after we moved to East Anglia, I became the area representative for Mission Aviation Fellowship (MAF) and have enjoyed speaking about the work in different churches. The mission started seventy years ago serving people living in remote areas in Africa, Papa New Guinea and parts of Asia. Today those places would take days to reach by roads, often impassable, while a plane can get there in twenty minutes with aid workers, medicines, food, eye specialists, dentists, etc. What many may not appreciate is that every three minutes of every day, except Sunday, a plane takes off or lands bringing much needed aid to vulnerable people somewhere.

And what of Arnie, the teacher who came along and I feel led me to Christ? Three years after he came, he left and went to work for African Inland Mission at a school in Jos, Nigeria. In the school, he met an Australian girl, a fellow teacher. They married and in 1984 they came to England on furlough. They came to see us with a little baby boy. Our second child was still a baby too. That was the last time I saw Arnie until 2014.

After 2010 I began to wonder where he was and contacted The Navigators—they said he was in Australia and they mailed him my email address. We exchanged Christmas newsletters and he invited us over to see them. What a joy to see them and to go to church with them! The sermon that morning was from Hebrews 13:7: "Remember your leaders who spoke the word of God to you." The preacher said these leaders were not church leaders nor pastors, they were the people who led you to Christ and spoke the word of God to you. I was sitting next to the man who did just that.

And what of our college friends, whom we stopped seeing when they told us they were expecting a baby? After we became Christians and had the two boys, I was listening to some preaching one morning about Joseph and his brothers and how they were reunited after all the sin committed. "We must contact John and Helen," I said to my wife. They were at the same address and we were reunited with them, had many meetings with them as their girls and our younger boys grew up and, in more recent years, we have had holidays together sharing sweet fellowship.

Lesson 1:

THE COST OF FOLLOWING JESUS

STILL QUITE A YOUNG CHRISTIAN, but enthusiastic about sharing my faith with young children from Muslim families, in 1979 I decided to do something in my classroom as Easter approached. I told the children the Easter story and how the Holy Spirit made the truth of it to me. In my zeal, I decided to fill the back wall of the classroom with a huge mural depicting Golgotha's hill with the three crosses prominent. I asked for three children to lie down on a big sheet of white paper to be drawn around for the figures to go on the crosses. The boy who went down for Jesus was a big well-built boy. Akbar was a troublesome bully who irritated other children. He was difficult to handle on occasions, but he wanted to lie down and so the figures were cut out and painted, then put on the three crosses.

I met Akbar several years later when he was at secondary school. It was after a parent's evening at our primary school. I was the last to leave. It was dark and as I wheeled my bicycle to the school door, I could just make out through the glass in the door, a large crowd of Muslim teenagers. They were blocking my way out. As I opened

24   My Teaching Days

the door I recognised Akbar, now nearly six feet tall and broad. For reasons unknown to me, they had angry, intense faces that made me fearful that they were going to attack me. I did not know if they were angry because of my faith or they were merely up to no good. I said firmly, "Excuse me, please," pushed my bike through the crowd, hopped onto it quickly and cycled off into the darkness. On the way home, I thought about the time Jesus simply walked through an angry mob, intent on killing him (Luke 4:28-30).

The next time I saw Akbar was a few years later in rather different circumstances. Our church was helping with a big tent mission in our local park. The week finished with a final rally held in the city Town Hall, a magnificent auditorium. I was invited to go along as a steward who was available to talk with anyone who wanted to enquire further after the meeting. After the gospel message and the final hymn, "Amazing Grace," I made my way to a room at the back. To my surprise, Akbar came into the room. The big young man looked rather tense. We recognised each other and he told me how a friend, a converted Muslim, had been witnessing to him, and had brought him along. He desperately wanted to know more about Jesus. Oh, that all of us should have that same desire! I took his phone number and for some time had contact with him till I felt he was in good hands. I felt he was in the best hands of all, the hands of one who would never leave him nor forsake him.

I left school about 5 p.m. one evening in 1987, work finished for the day. I packed some books into the paniers on my bicycle and got ready to cycle home. Out of the school gate and down the road, I passed a building which had been converted into a mosque. Many of the children in the area were picked up after school in mini-buses and driven to this mosque for lessons in the Quran. As I approached the building, I saw such a mini-bus driving in my direction. I was certainly not prepared for what happened next.

The mini-bus veered from its side of the road and was coming towards me. I quickly turned my bicycle off the road towards some factory on my right, jumped off my bike and avoided the bus by a small margin. I saw the children in the bus half-standing pointing at me, and talking to the driver. Then the bus got back onto its side of the road and sped off into the distance. Were some of those children ones who came to our school and did they point me out to the driver as one who believed in Jesus? I thought of Peter warming himself before the fire when a servant girl exclaimed, "You too were with Him! "

The cost of following Jesus.

Lesson 2

CHANGING ATTITUDES ABOUT COMPETITION

I HAVE ALWAYS ENJOYED PLAYING competitive games such as football, cricket, golf or tennis. As a boy and a young man and before I became a Christian, I was a terrible loser and could not control my mouth if I lost. I argued with the referee and always blamed someone else rather than accepting my own bad skills or mistakes. When I began teaching I loved encouraging children to play sports and oversaw the boy's football team. However, my attitude was not right. When I took the team to play another school, I could not control my tongue if we were losing.

When the Spirit of God began working in me, I began to change. The Spirit gave me better self-control. I saw nothing wrong with competitive games, what was wrong had been my attitude. I tried to encourage children to control themselves, not to blame anyone when they got things wrong, and to accept they needed to work hard to improve their own skills. I began to understand what the Apostle Paul meant when he said in 1 Corinthians 9:24, "I run the race as if only one gets the prize." He didn't compare himself, he didn't blame anyone else and he worked hard to improve himself and be the best. This was Joseph's attitude in Potiphar's house. He gained promotion, Potiphar's property and gardens, all that he owned were blessed by God. Joseph was running a race to be the best. So, too, were Daniel and his friends and all the Old Testament witnesses. This was the Protestant work ethic which made England great in Victorian days. Competition is not wrong. Children will always thrive when they have something to aim for and compete to be the best. This applies to work with pen and paper in the classroom too. Good, clearly defined aims to work for, marking with scores whenever possible and regular testing. In his second letter to the Corinthians in chapter 13, Paul urges them in verse 5: "Examine yourselves to see whether you are in the faith, test yourselves." He tells Timothy to test himself and 1 Timothy 6:12 writes: "Fight the good fight of the faith."

Unfortunately, soon after I became a Christian, in the 1970s, '80s, '90s, and probably so today still, there were philosophies taking over in education which fed the idea that competition was evil, distinctions in toys and games for boys and girls were also wrong. Children should be in charge of their own learning, and discover at their own rate skills in reading, writing and numbers. Instead of skills being taught with clearly defined goals to aim for, children were to somehow discover the skills. Marking became vague with comments like "very well tried" on all pieces of work. Ideas and play apparati were devised in which boys and girls together could participate with supposedly no competition. In the classroom desks were joined together so children could sit in groups and discuss work together. My own observations of this approach were that children chattered all the time, and often about nothing to do with the task in hand.

Changing Attitudes about Competition   29

I personally kept my desks in rows facing the front with two children at a desk working in silence. The children loved it, got on with their own work, worked hard, minding their own business, annoying no one. I introduced competition in most subjects, giving marks for good work. In maths, where answers were either right or wrong it was easier to give a score and the children loved getting them to see how well they had done. It spurred them on to get as few wrong as possible. In literacy, I always told them what the marks would be awarded for. If it was creative writing I might say, for example, that I was looking for capital letters and full-stops in the right places, plus some very good adjectives used and sentences beginning with good connectives. There would be additional marks for good, neat handwriting. The children knew what they were aiming for and were eager to see how well they had done.

I loved teaching spelling. The children were in four ability groups, and to each group I gave eight new spellings, all using the same letters to make a particular sound, every week. The spelling test on Friday morning had 15 spellings for each group. Eight of them would be the new ones and seven would be taken from the previous weeks to ensure they had not been forgotten. After lunch on Friday, they were most eager to hear the scores. I read them out and kept the best five till last. Sometimes a lower ability child got the top score of 15, but I never heard a more able child say, "but they had easier ones." They all wanted to get the best score.

They enjoyed it and the work improved. We were all asked, from time to time, to send in sample work from different levels of ability in each subject, so that the headteacher and subject leader could check on how children were achieving. When the subject leader returned

30 My Teaching Days

my books, they expressed with a gasp how good they were compared with other classes. It encouraged me to know that the methods I was employing did produce results.

The writer to the Hebrews, I believe it to be Paul, after he has recorded the exploits of saints of old in chapter 11, begins chapter 12 with these words:

"Since we are surrounded by such a great cloud of witnesses, let us throw off everything that hinders and the sin that so easily entangles and let us run with perseverance the race marked out for us. Let us fix our eyes on Jesus the author and perfecter of our faith."

The enemy is working relentlessly to discourage us, to cause us to give up, and children need much encouragement to succeed and reach their best. Good marking with scores and regular testing, I believe, can help them see whether they are improving and reaching the goal for which they are striving. In a former age, these methods worked well. If applied well, they still today will foster a right spirit. It is the same spirit which inspired Caleb, Joseph, Daniel, the Apostle Paul, indeed all the saints of old.

Competition, marking, scores, testing are not wrong. I am glad my dentist worked hard to acquire skills, was tested and marked. Because of this I can trust him. I still use these methods though now retired. In Beccles Grace Baptist Church I attend is a young man in his twenties with some learning difficulties. He is growing as a Christian. A year ago, I asked if he would like to improve his spelling. I first tested him to find a level. One morning every week I give him a test with 30 spellings. If he scores 25 or more I give him eight new words having the same sound in them. Over the course of the year he has had several new groups of words to learn. He works very hard not to go below 20. The scoring is key. He loves the challenge and is competing only against himself, not comparing himself with anyone else. He's learning Scripture too.

Again Paul, writing to the Galatians, in 6:3-5 says these words, "If anyone thinks he is something when he is nothing, he deceives himself. Each one should test his own actions. Then he can take pride in himself, without comparing himself to somebody else, for each one should carry his own load."

In verse 9, he writes, "Let us not become weary in doing good, for at the proper time we will reap a harvest if we do not give up."

At the beginning of this article I stated as a boy and young person I couldn't control my tongue. I also struggled with other sins. So, whenever I encouraged pupils to do the right thing, I also told them that as a boy I was probably more badly behaved than they were.

"What did you get up to, sir?" they asked.

I simply said, "Jesus has forgiven every one of them. I'm still not perfect, but He still forgives me."

Lesson 3

TANGIBLE POWER

I ARRIVED AT SCHOOL EARLY one morning in 1968 to be told that the person due to take assembly that morning was off sick and there would be no assembly unless someone was prepared to fill in. I could see a few disappointed faces, so I instantly offered. It was a morning when all the teachers did not need to come in and could have some free time. I sensed the Spirit of God leading and the story to tell would be Elijah and the prophets of Baal on Mount Carmel, partly told and partly read from my Bible so that the children could see where it came from. 300 faces had their eyes on me. The story has some good touches of humour as Elijah taunts the false prophets and an exciting climax, too, as Elijah races down the mountain after rain has come. It also revealed the one true God. The prophets of Baal did everything they could to make their god act, even to the point of cutting themselves. He did not respond. Elijah only prayed, even pouring water on the sacrifice. The true God answered with resounding power. How I prayed that the children would be touched by the Spirit to see the difference between the gods of the world who demand so much from us and never respond and the eternal God of Grace who

34   My Teaching Days

made a bigger sacrifice than the prophets and Elijah set up when He gave His only Son. Most of the staff were glad that I had led the assembly and as the day went on I noticed children staring at me, with wide eyes as I walked past.

What was to follow, as I look back, found me standing in awe. That evening my wife and I went to a Bible study in someone's home. We were interrupted several times by loud cracks of thunder and lightning flashes every few seconds. We could hear rain pounding against the windows. This must be heard all over the city, I thought. The next morning was fairer as I cycled to school. It was my policy when the children came in to stand at a certain point in the corridor and make sure that the children walked along in single file in an orderly manner. That morning, as the children passed me, one by one they turned sideways to look with seemingly frightened eyes at me, backing away from me as far as they could to the opposite wall and then shuffling on down the corridor never taking their eyes off me. One by one they did this till all had passed. The story of Elijah, then the electric storm that evening. God has spoken, I thought, God has spoken.

Lesson 4

THE NEED FOR PRAYER

THE APOSTLE PAUL WROTE IN 2 Corinthians 6:

"We put no obstacle in anyone's way, so that no fault may be found with our ministry, but as servants of God we commend ourselves in every way: by great endurance, in afflictions, hardships, calamities, beatings, imprisonments, riots, labors, sleepless nights, hunger; by purity, knowledge, patience, kindness, the Holy Spirit, genuine love; by truthful speech, and the power of God; with the weapons of righteousness for the right hand and for the left; through honor and dishonor, through slander and praise. We are treated as impostors, and yet are true; as unknown, and yet well known; as dying, and behold, we live; as punished, and yet not killed; as sorrowful, yet always rejoicing; as poor, yet making many rich; as having nothing, yet possessing everything."

At my own toughest times in the teaching profession, similar to those described in 2 Corinthians 6, I was very grateful to be weekly meeting with five or six Christian brothers for an early morning Bible study and prayer time. We met in someone's home at 6:30 a.m. for about 45 minutes. I was the only teacher, but not the only one facing difficulties. We took weekly turns to share a short passage of

36   My Teaching Days

Scripture and a few thoughts about it before we shared our needs and problems and spent time laying them before God in prayer. The person leading for the week also prepared six cards on which was written the key verse from the passage. We each took a card and pledged to memorise the verse for the next meeting. I cannot overemphasise the importance of this. In John 14:26, Jesus said, "But the Counsellor, the Holy Spirit whom the Father will send in my name will teach you and will bring to your remembrance everything I have said to you." A wise old teacher I once heard preaching on this verse said, "How can the Spirit bring back to your remembrance what you have not remembered in the first place?" He was stressing the importance of memorising Scripture with the brilliant minds we have been given.

The psalmist, too, knew the value of this as he wrote in Psalm 119:11: "I have hidden your word in my heart that I might not sin against you."

Jeremiah wrote in 15:16: "When your words came I ate them, they were my joy and my heart's delight."

And Jesus, Himself, when tempted by the devil in the wilderness in Matthew 4:1-11, answered each temptation with the words, "It is written . . ."

I began to think as Scripture says, "we are fearfully made." I began to think that includes an incredible brain with a wonderful capacity to remember all kinds of information. I still can remember nursery rhymes from infancy, no use or help to anyone. I remember multiplication tables from early days. I don't practise remembering them ever but if anyone asked me 7x9 I could give the answer immediately. No excuses for not memorising Scripture, and how much more profitable to remember John 3:16 and many more promises. I felt convicted after reading 1 John 5:14-15: "This is the confidence we have in approaching God, that if we ask anything according to His will, he hears us. And if we know that he hears us – whatever we ask– we know that we have what we asked of Him." I began to reason that the more we memorised His will, the more confidence we could have in approaching Him.

Those early mornings once a week with those men were very profitable. We pledged ourselves to memorise more of His will in Scripture and some of those verses I still remember today. And when any of us was facing a difficult, problematic day which could have caused great anxiety, we knew the others would be praying even beyond our early morning meeting. They would be praying at other times of the day confident of His promise, "Cast all your cares on me for I care about you."

Lesson 5

THE MISSING KEY

THE YEAR 4 CLASS I had in the 1980s was a good class. They responded well to my teachings with good, careful, well-presented work. They also listened well to Bible stories I told them and watched eagerly the film of Patricia St. John's "Treasures of the Snow" which I showed to them at Christmas. There were even cries of "where can we buy this, sir?" I emphasised the doctrine of forgiveness, pointing out that the God of the Bible was kind and forgiving. Hard working though they were, there were a few of the children who could not be trusted. They were light-fingered and could be known to steal items from other children and not own up. At playtimes, some would be known to find an excuse, put to the teacher on duty outside, to come back into school for something. Once inside they would try a few classroom doors and if one was open, go inside to steal. Some were caught.

As we approached playtime one day, I searched for my classroom key ready to let the children out to play, then lock the door. I could not find it. I searched drawers, my table full of papers and books with no success. As the bell went for play I felt I could not let the children out. I felt sure one of them had it and could use it to get into other

40   My Teaching Days

classrooms since all used the same key. I stood sternly at the front while the children sat in silence. After a while I suggested that if anyone had the key, they could quietly put it on the floor beside their desk, then look down and suddenly announce they had found it. There was no response. Only more silence as I stood before them with one hand in my jacket pocket. Aghast, as my fingers fiddled with some papers in the pocket, I felt the classroom key. My first thought was to keep the children a little longer then let the children out for the few remaining minutes of playtime to go to the toilet. I would stay in the room and when the children came back in, I would announce that I had searched further and had found the key. Immediately I heard the voice of the Holy Spirit saying, "Do not lie, tell them the truth now." My first reaction was to say, "No, I can't do that," but He said, "Tell them the truth now!"

With a quaking voice, I stumbled over the words, "Children I want to tell you the truth. I've just had my hand in my pocket and my classroom key is there. I'm sorry, please forgive me."

I will never forget what happened next. Twenty-five smiling faces were looking at me and with almost one voice they said together, "We forgive you, sir."

I wanted, like Joseph when he met his brothers, to dash into my stockroom and cry. Later I thought about Jesus teaching on the Mount in Matthew 5:8: "Blessed are the pure in heart for they will see God." I was also reminded of the words in John's gospel in 3:21: "But whoever lives by the truth comes into the light so that it may be seen plainly that what he has done has been done through God." How important I felt it was to present such teaching in action to my school children.

Lesson 6

THE TRIBUNAL

IN 1987, A NEW HEADTEACHER was appointed to the school who was an advisor to the city education committee on multi-faith and multi-culturalism. She picked up the fact that when I had to take an assembly, I always did a Bible story or a Bible theme and began by quoting some words of Jesus from the Bible. At Christmas, I had to conduct the assembly telling the story of Christ's birth, using slides from the Jesus of Nazareth film. With each slide, I read the appropriate words from a Bible I held so that the children and their parents could see where the commentary was coming from.

One day she called me in to talk about my views on multi-faith education. I explained that I believed that there was only one true faith so how could there be any other, and that I could only teach the Christian faith. Becoming a little aggressive, she told me that I would have to teach other faiths, or she would call in our area inspector and I would have to face a tribunal hearing, perhaps being dismissed. I was given a few days to think this over.

I arranged to meet with several of my Christian brothers in the church for prayer and advice. One or two advised that I should agree

42   My Teaching Days

to teach other faiths and say to the children that though some believed it, I, personally, did not, but I was a Christian. But as I pondered this I thought that to do it this way would give the impression to young children that because some believed it, then it could be considered another plausible and acceptable way to God. One or two others suggested that I should look at good things in other faiths which were also dealt with in the Bible. But I felt that Christianity is not about good works first and foremost. I knew well the verses in Ephesians 2 "for by grace you have been saved through faith, and this is not from yourselves, it is the gift of God—not by works so that no one can boast." The next verse goes on to explain that we are God's workmanship, created in Christ Jesus for good works which He prepared in advance for us to do. So, if He prepared them, He alone must have all the glory and none other. I also knew that in both the Old and New Testament God had said that we must be holy as He is holy in the sense that He is totally devoted to us as a loving Heavenly Father and we should be devoted to Him and His will alone.

To be fair, I felt that that some of these brothers were thinking of my wife and two young children, since they would be affected with my job loss. But my Lord's will is greater and I could not teach other faiths, and I had to go back a few days later and tell the headteacher of my decision. She had already been in touch with an inspector and told me I would have to go to meet with three chief inspectors in city council offices and explain my position. I decided to face it alone, but not entirely alone. I knew that from my conversion the Holy Spirit lives in me. I had lain on my heart Jesus' words in Luke's gospel in 21:12-15: "But before all this, they will seize you and persecute you. They will hand you over to synagogues and put you in prison, and you will be brought before kings and governors, and all on account of my name. And so you will bear testimony to me. But make up your mind not to worry beforehand how you will defend yourselves. For I will give you words and wisdom that none of your adversaries will be able to resist or contradict."

I had also committed to memory years before this incident verses from Philippians 4:5b-7: "The Lord is near. Do not be anxious about anything, but in every situation, by prayer and petition, with thanksgiving, present your requests to God. And the peace of God, which transcends all understanding, will guard your hearts and your minds in Christ Jesus."

I was grateful for that area of the Holy Spirit's ministry in bringing this Scripture back to memory, as well as other comforting Scriptures. I had to wait a couple of weeks for the hearing and I am saying that at times I had some anxiety. I am human and still have a sinful nature but the Spirit fights to have control of me and I lost no sleep the night before the tribunal. I did not tell my wife, not wanting to cause her the pain of worrying.

In the offices that morning I was called into a room to be faced by the three inspectors, one my own school area inspector—an atheist, one a Sikh, one a Hindu. They asked me why I would not teach other faiths. I replied, "Jesus said, 'I am the way, the truth and the life, no one comes to the Father except through me.'" Outraged, they told me that I would have to resign immediately. I replied that I would not and that they would have to fire me. There was silence and then I was asked to leave and go back to my work at school, not a very easy thing to do.

44 My Teaching Days

I heard nothing for weeks, then our area school inspector visited the school. He came into my classroom with bad news, I thought, but he said that he was just visiting and looked at children's work, talked to them and then left with words of praise for what he had seen. A few months later I heard that he had left the authority and taken a job in another area. Within 18 months the headteacher decided to leave. I never did teach any other so-called faiths and I felt sure the children respected me for this. Their parents also had more respect for someone who stood up for what he believed than for those who said it doesn't matter what you believe, because for them it did. I continued on in the school for a number of years and was blessed when two Christian ladies joined the staff. One was a converted Hindu, the other an evangelical Anglican whose husband worked for a Scripture union and often visited the school to lead assemblies. The lady converted from Hinduism was eager to share her faith and one day I overheard her reading Isaiah 53 with the new headteacher. After the tribunal, there were many good days when I felt God's Spirit moving in glorious ways.

I went with Satpal to lunchtime meetings of local Christians. She and I had many good discussions about supernatural activity. We both were aware of 2 Corinthians 4:4: "The god of this age has blinded the minds of unbelievers so that they cannot see the light of the gospel of the glory of Christ who is the image of God." We both agreed that it takes a supernatural work of God's Holy Spirit to make a person alive with Christ Jesus and all the believers agreed that God alone must have all the glory for any conversion.

I am conscious that still today there may be many teachers facing the situations I faced. I have met some of them in my travels. The area I now live in, far from any big city, introduced into the Religious Education syllabus "humanism" while I was doing some supply teaching a few years ago. It is still in the curriculum and teachers are being asked to teach it. Every morning in my quiet time with the Lord, after praying for my believing family, I begin with earnest prayer for nearly 20 Christian teachers who I know value prayer.

Lesson 7

THE HUMAN HEART

AT MY CONVERSION, I WAS convicted of where my biggest problem lay—and the biggest problem all people have—the human heart. In Jeremiah 17:9-10a I learned it is "deceitful above all things and beyond cure. Who can understand it? I, the Lord, search the heart and examine the mind." In Mark 7:21-23, Jesus says, "For it is from within, out of a person's heart, that evil thoughts come—sexual immorality, theft, murder, adultery, greed, malice, deceit, lewdness, envy, slander, arrogance and folly. All these evils come from inside and defile a person." It became clear to me once I became a child of God that I was in a battle for my very soul, that every thought, every word, every action, every look and every deed had its root beginning within my sinful heart and it was a battle to keep it pure. A wise proverb was written on my heart in Proverbs 4:23: "Above all else, guard your heart, for everything you do flows from it." David knew that battle and that he could never create a clean heart within him. You, alone can do it, O God. "Create in me, O God a clean heart" he prayed. I, too, needed my heart sprinkled with the blood of the lamb in those early days of my Christian walk and I still have that need today.

48   My Teaching Days

Children have not kept their hearts pure, no one has. I loved teaching mathematics, particularly mental arithmetic. With young children, I thought handling money would be a natural way to improve mental skills. I pointed out how helpful it would be in shops. If they gave a £1 coin to a shopkeeper, they would know immediately whether they had received the correct change. It was very important if they didn't want to be cheated. I would illustrate this point with a true story of when my wife and I bought some sandwiches in a shop once. My wife handed over a £10 note and the assistant gave her the change. Immediately, my wife called to the retreating assistant, "Excuse me, but you have given me the wrong change," for she could calculate it in two seconds. When the assistant said, "Let me look," my wife said, "you have given me a £1 too much," and gave the coin back. You can probably guess what nearly all the children shouted out every time I told the story: "I would have kept it." Such is the human heart.

With this in mind, I found myself in a difficult situation at the end of every term. It was the custom of one member of staff to bring in a video of a film to play on the big television set we had and to invite all classes in the upper school to come and watch. The thought that troubled my mind was that at the beginning of each video was a warning that it should not be used in places like schools, only homes. I knew verses in Scripture like Ephesians 5:11 that say, "Have nothing to do with the fruitless deeds of darkness, but rather expose them. It is shameful even to mention what the disobedient do in secret."

So I explained the truth of what I knew about the warnings and told them I would not force them to go to watch, even though I knew I could have two hours of free time if I did. I had some good

THE HUMAN HEART   49

skill-based games and offered them as an alternative. Each time, nearly all the children chose this option.

In 1988, I found myself in the position of wanting to show a video. I had a very hard-working class of children who worked quietly and got on well with each other. During the year, I had read to them a shortened version of the story, "The Railway Children" by E. Nesbit, and in the final term I thought it would be good to show the children the delightful film based on the book, but I could not in my heart defy the warning at the beginning of the film. So, I found a U.K. telephone number for Warner Bros. and rang them. A kind gentleman said that he would have loved to be able to say he could waive the warning, but he could not and he left it to my conscience—it was licenced only for home use.

A Christian lady, converted from Hinduism, was helping me in class each week. For a couple of hours, I discussed the situation with her. She suggested a way she could possibly help. She was friendly with a missionary couple, now into their last assignment and coming to work in the multi-racial area near the school. They had purchased a large Victorian house nearby and were not planning to move in for a few weeks. They had put in a little furniture, including a television set. She could get the keys from them and my class could walk down to the house and watch in a home. I thought I had better check this out with Warner Bros. and spoke again to the same gentleman who assured me that this way would be fine. It was being used in a home. Absurd as the rule of law seemed, before God I felt my conscience and my heart was pure.

It was a fine day. We walked them down to the house. My friend had brought in squash and nibbles for the interval, and the children enjoyed the morning and listened as I told them all I had done to keep my heart pure before God on the matter.

Lesson 8

PROVIDENCE AND SOVEREIGNTY

WHEN I BECAME A BELIEVER forty years ago, one of the first doctrines I came to understand was the providence of God. The school I was working in was fast becoming nearly one-hundred percent Asian with children from Muslim, Sikh and Hindu parents. I questioned what I was doing there, being the only Christian. However, we were going through the story of Joseph on Sunday mornings and I could see that he must have felt the same as I did, a stranger and alien in the world. But as the story unfolds, Joseph is reunited with his brothers in a surprising turn of events and declares to them the wonder of God's providence.

In Genesis 45:5-8a, it says, "And now do not be distressed and angry with yourselves for selling me here, because it was to save lives that God sent me ahead of you. For two years now there has been famine in the land and for the next five years there will not be ploughing or reaping. But God sent me ahead of you to preserve for you a remnant on earth and to save your lives by a great deliverance. So, then, it was not you who sent me here, but God."

52 My Teaching Days

I was also reading through the Acts of the Apostles and when I came to 17:26 with Paul in Athens, I read these words: "From one man he made all the nations, that they should inhabit the whole earth; and he marked out their appointed times in history and the boundaries of their lands."

As Joseph trusted in God's faithful, providential hand, I decided I would do the same. If God wanted me there He must have a purpose and as I look back, I can see the ways in which God used me. From that early point in my Christian walk, I gave up believing in luck or fortunes. So many difficult circumstances and near catastrophes have happened in my teaching career, but as I look back I have been delivered from them all, often by surprising turns of events which I never put down to chance or good luck. Rather, I have learned to trust in the merciful, gracious, powerful, kind, forgiving, overseeing and wise hand of God.

I also, around the same time, came to a firm belief in the first three chapters of Genesis. I never taught evolutionary ideas, that the earth was created by a series of random events but that God created all things. I saw the children I taught as made in the image of God. All the classes I taught heard the Genesis 3 account of the fall of man and an explanation of all evil and wickedness in the world. I stressed the importance of not blaming anyone else when they did something wrong as Adam and Eve both did. The children, like many down the ages, often tried to worm out of personal responsibility by blaming someone else. Social workers will blame upbringing, politicians will blame living in poverty. Never did Genesis 3 come into the picture for bad behaviour.

Providence and Sovereignty 53

Closely linked to God's providence, I learned about God's sovereignty. He knows those He chooses. Acts 13:48 says, "all those who were appointed for eternal life, believed," after hearing of salvation. I would say it was not a surprise to God when I came to believe. He wasn't shocked.

Some of my students built a snowman for a competition.

I became aware of how to view those around me, the staff, some of whom were Muslims, and the pupils from different Asian countries. In 2 Corinthians 5:16-19, Paul writes about how he saw the people around him: "So from now on we regard no one from a worldly point of view. Though we once regarded Christ in this way we do so no longer. Therefore, if anyone be in Christ he is a new creation, the old has gone, the new is here! All this is from God who reconciled us to Himself through Christ and gave us the ministry of reconciliation that God was reconciling the world to Himself in Christ, not counting people's sins against them. And He has committed to us the ministry of reconciliation."

Paul is looking at people, whom he sees in the flesh, to see if they can testify about any spiritual renewal, if they are a new creation, not living now according to the pattern of the world and of the flesh. And this was how I viewed the staff and pupils around me. Paul makes it clear the supernatural reasons why they remained lost and dead to God, dead in trespasses and sins in 2 Corinthians 4:3-4: "And even if our gospel is veiled it is veiled to those who are perishing. The God of this age has blinded unbelievers, so they cannot see the light of the gospel of the glory of Christ, who is the image of God."

In Ephesians 2:6-8, only God who is rich in mercy, can make us alive in Christ Jesus and raise us up and seat us with him in the heavenly realms, a supernatural work no man can do. With all this in mind I led many assemblies, had many conversations with staff, never pushing the gospel at them, but allowing them to ask questions. One of the most interesting times was working in a Year 5 group with a Hindu and a Christadelphian, who asked many questions about my faith. Children allowed me to read from the Bible to them. How powerful is the Word of God! They were willing to talk about what they believed and allowed me to share gently what I believed on topics such as facing God on the day of judgement. None of this happened by chance. I was regularly meeting with some men for prayer and I asked for prayer that God would open some doors for me to be able to share good portions from His word. He certainly did that and so I saw the providential hand of God at work many times.

Lesson 9

MINISTRY DURING CHRISTMASTIME

THE SCHOOL ALWAYS DID A Christmas show to which parents were invited. Because the area was over 90 percent Muslim it was never a carol concert with Bible readings. One year in the 1990s, my year group was given the task of planning the event and I, the leader of the group, had to suggest ideas. I took an idea from a Scripture Union book and adapted and developed it my own way. We built a time machine, using some school furniture and cardboard boxes, complete with flashing lights when the machine landed. Two children were travellers who could go through a door into the machine and go back in time. I told the headteacher that I wanted to include a nativity scene and one or two carols, and to explain simply why Jesus came.

To my surprise she was enthusiastic about the nativity scenes and offered to get some costumes for shepherds and wise men from a school she knew. The idea was that the two travellers would travel back to different periods of history, first to a time in the first World War when, during Christmas, fighting in the trenches stopped and soldiers on both sides came together, sang "Silent Night" and had a game of football. Then, there was an early Victorian family scene with another carol. Next, back to a Tudor street scene of festivities, and finally back to the Nativity. For each scene, the two travellers stepped out of the machine to observe what was happening.

As the machine travelled back through time its lights flashed and a tape played. A good Christian friend who knew a bit about audio, helped me produce the tape. Recording first the music "Finlandia" by Sibelius, over the loud crescendo building up to the quiet melody to which the words, "I Rest on Thee My Shield and My Defender," were put, he superimposed my echoing voice counting down the years in tens or hundreds, depending on the gap. When the correct year was reached the door of the machine opened to the quiet melody. When we reached year zero the quiet tune to "I Rest on Thee" played on a little longer as Joseph and Mary walked across the stage to the inn. When the nativity scene was finished, the two travellers walked slowly back to the machine. Once inside their voices could be heard talking about why Jesus came.

Later that week a teacher, not a believer, came up to me and said, "That tune you kept playing as the machine landed, isn't that the tune of an old hymn? Obviously, it rang a bell and God may have used other parts of the production to

A model of wise men bringing gifts to Jesus made by 10 year olds in my early teaching days.

Ministry During Christmastime   57

convict souls of truths which will never pass away. To Him, alone, be all the glory.

One Christmas my class had to take part in a Christmas assembly to which parents were invited, mainly Muslims. I decided to do a poem I found in an old poetry book called "The Golden Book of Children's Verse" by Frank Jones, long out of print and out of print when I used it. The poem was entitled "Little Gottlieb" by Phoebe Cary. The narrative would be read by different groups of children in unison. Individual children would mime the narrative and read the words spoken by different characters.

Set in Germany it tells the story of a little boy, living alone with his mother, who worked hard to provide for them both. Gottlieb often sat beside his mother and pondered. When he became a man, he thought of all the wonderful things he would for do her. But,

"It was only a week till Christmas

and Gottlieb knew that then,

the Christ child who was born that day

sent down good gifts to men."

Gottlieb decided to write a letter to the Christ child. The baffled postmaster doesn't know what to do with it, so takes it to the wise burgomaster, who, equally baffled opens it and stands dismayed:

"That such a little child should dare

to ask the Lord for aid."

Christmas morning comes and Gottlieb rises early to find his mother standing with the burgomaster beside her. The hearth is full

58 My Teaching Days

of logs and the table filled with fine food. The burgomaster takes full credit and tells Gottlieb that his letter did not get to the Christ child but to him. The burgomaster addresses the child:

"T'was a foolish thing you did,

as you must understand,

For though the gifts are yours, you know,

You have them from my hand."

But Gottlieb has the final word.

"Then Gottlieb answered fearlessly

where he humbly stood apart.

"But the Christ child sent them all the same

He put the thought in your heart."

The children enjoyed doing this and lots of good seed was sown during rehearsals.

Every Christmas was an opportunity to show the children a film such as "Treasures of The Snow," "Tanglewood Secrets," or the excellent cartoon version of "The Lion, The Witch and The Wardrobe." The children loved these and after one showing of "Treasures of The Snow," some of the children asked where they could buy the video. One or two said, "no, our parents say we are not to listen to anything about Jesus."

Another good gospel film I came across through the excellent video lending library of the Birmingham City Mission was a Heinz Fuzzle production called "More than A Champion." One Church of England school I went to asked if I would do the call of Moses to go to

Pharaoh and the following week to do something about the meaning of Easter. I loved the challenge of this and the Lord helped me greatly, so the next session I had with them before the Easter break I asked if I could show the film "More than A Champion" to them. The film shows some of the meaning of Easter through the eyes of a young boy.

When in full time teaching during the 1980s and 1990s, I was asked to do both the Christmas story and the Easter story using slides from the BBC "Jesus of Nazareth" series. The script I took word for word from the NIV accounts. Another member of staff changed the slides, so that I could deliver the script with meaning and conviction in my voice. The story at Christmas was interspersed with carols. In the Easter story I used music from Roger Jones' "Jerusalem Joy" such as "Jesus Rode a Donkey into Town." I was amazed that God opened a door for me to do this as the school was over ninety percent Muslim children, and also morning assemblies had changed considerably over the years since I began in the school. When I began, I had not yet become a Christian, though I perhaps thought I was. So, I approved the assemblies in those early days, late '60s and early '70s. The children all took a hymn book into assembly, sang songs such as "Loving Shepherd of Thy Sheep," and "All Glory, Laud and Honour." The head-teacher would then read a story from a children's Bible. By the 1980s, after I had become a Christian, I was amazed that God heard the prayers of several Christian friends and myself so that I was able to do the Christmas and Easter stories with meaning throughout the '80s and '90s.

Lesson 10

A DIFFICULT YEAR

JESUS SAID IN JOHN 15:18, 20: "If the world hates you, keep in mind that it hated me first . . . if they persecuted me, they will persecute you also." Paul also warned Timothy in 2 Timothy 3:12 that "everyone who wants to live a godly life in Christ Jesus will be persecuted." Despite these promises, I was rather shocked when it came. In 1990 I was given a Year 6 class of 11-year-old children, of mainly Muslim background. Many of the children I knew a little of because I had taught their older brothers or sisters in earlier years. Their older siblings would have gone home to tell of some Bible stories I had told in class or in assembly. They might have talked about films I tended to show around Christmas. From the first day I had this class, I felt opposition and hatred. The children would not look at me when I spoke to them and they turned their faces away defiantly. They put little effort into the work and occasionally I would hear a cry from somewhere in the room "kill Jesus, kill Jesus." I struggled with wanting to be there in the mornings.

As the term went on, I decided to send a note to the headteacher. Foolishly, I told the children I had asked the headteacher to come to

62 My Teaching Days

my classroom and about the attitude to work. When she came, the children were working well, putting up their hands, eagerly answering questions and looking at me. She could see nothing wrong. She was not a Christian and I felt that she would not understand even if I told her everything that had been going on.

There was no one to turn to in the school who would have understood or even cared, and I have since learned of many teachers in a similar position. The only people to whom I could turn to for help were the group of Christian brothers I met weekly for early morning prayer. One would share a passage of Scripture for encouragement and we would pray. I shared everything with them. What a blessing that was to me as they prayed for me! The power of prayer is not so much in the one praying as in the One to whom we are praying.

The year went on with little improvement, but the children knew that I loved sport as many of them did. They knew that in the spring and summer, on warmer days, I would give my children an extra games lesson outside in the spacious playgrounds, but only if the children worked really hard during the week.

It grieved them to do so, but the work improved when warmer weather came and they made an effort to respond to me and sometimes even look at me. So, because I love sport and because I never stopped loving them—Jesus said to love your enemies, pray for them that persecute you—I gave them some extra games lessons. Still they remained aloof from me and sometimes going down to assembly, I would feel a child's hand pushing something into mine— an anti-Christian tract.

The year ended and on the last day they left quickly without any goodbyes as they passed me. I thanked the Lord that I had somehow survived the year.

Some years later, on a sunny summer afternoon, I was playing outside with a more pleasant class. As the game went on, I turned and noticed two young ladies walking towards me. I recognised them as the difficult twins I had tried to teach in that difficult year. They must have been 17 or 18 years old. They slowly walked up to me and I noticed tears coming.

"We're sorry, sir. We're sorry," they uttered in trembling voices.

I wanted to cry. "You are forgiven," I said, trembling too. "You can know that. You are forgiven."

How the Spirit of God moves I know not!

Lesson 11

TEACHING ABOUT SIN WITH MATH LESSONS

AT THE END OF A math lesson, when there was some time before the bell, I liked to set children a mental challenge. One time, picking out one of the boys who had been a little disruptive, I said, "If Robert here only does one thing wrong each day in the eyes of God, who sees everything, how many wrong things will he have done in a week?"

Someone called out, "Robert does more than one thing wrong every day. He does lots!"

"But if he does *only* one wrong thing every day how many in a week?"

"Seven, sir."

I then added, "Ok, if he keeps that up for a whole year, how many would that be?"

"365, sir."

I continued: "Well Robert is now ten years old. How many wrong things so far at one a day?" Not so many hands went up, but eventually I received an answer,

66 My Teaching Days

"3650, sir."

"Now how many by the time he's twenty years old?"

We then went on to thirty, forty and fifty years old. A good mental arithmetic filler, but then with a few minutes left I added, "Well I've certainly done more than one thing wrong every day. Now suppose I get knocked off my bicycle on the way home and I am killed. I stand before God, and it looks bad for me, all the things not done the way God wanted me to live. I'm guilty and should be punished, no hope of heaven. But someone stands beside me who can take my punishment. Jesus did no wrong, but He took my punishment on the cross where He died. He took the punishment for anyone who will believe."

"I have believed," I tell the children, "no punishment for me. Heaven for me."

Lesson 12

CHOOSING MY WORDS

I HAD BEEN WELL TAUGHT as a young Christian on the Protestant work ethic and upon obeying leaders. I wrote on my heart Scriptures such as Ephesians 6:5-7: "Slaves, obey your earthly masters with respect and fear and with sincerity of heart just as you would obey Christ. Obey them, not only to win their favour when their eye is on you, but like slaves of Christ, doing the will of God from your heart, serve wholeheartedly as if you were serving the Lord, not people." I read the great stories of Abraham, Moses, Joshua, Caleb, Joseph, Daniel, Elijah, Elisha, Nehemiah, Peter, Paul and all the Saints surrounding us. They lived out the words of Scripture, they were bold, fearless, hard-working, unashamed, insulted, mocked, even prepared to die for the sake of the One who had saved them and called them to serve Him alone.

And so, when I became a believer, my attitudes changed in many areas. I prepared work well, I marked children's work more carefully. Some work was difficult to read and sometimes when I got to the sixteenth book in a pile of 33 and saw work too difficult to read or make anything of, I was tempted not to bother, just put a tick and a

68   My Teaching Days

comment such as 'well tried,' but the Spirit would always say "no" and then show me ways I could constructively help that child. Gradually I began to see improvement in all the children, for most of whom English was a second language. All praise and thanks to the Spirit who was leading me.

Another area which had to change was my speech and attitude in the staffroom. Most playtimes and lunch breaks were an opportunity for someone to slander someone who was absent. Chiefly, it was the headteacher. Others would join in and sometimes the comments made behind her back, I felt, had some justification. Before my conversion I would have eagerly joined in the mud-slinging. But now I needed the Spirit of God to help me control my thoughts and my tongue. Some staff members looked at me in wonder. Why was I not joining in? I felt for the headteacher. She was aware of what was going on and, occasionally, she would burst into the staffroom, hoping to catch someone in full flow. Staff would stop in mid-sentence and there would be a sudden silence as she entered. I longed to be able to tell her that I was not joining in.

Around this time, I was listening to preaching from 1 Samuel. I was challenged by how David responded to Saul's hatred of him. Saul was chasing after David, having been told he was in the wilderness of En Gedi. He takes 3,000 men then in 1 Samuel 24:3-6, " . . . he came to the sheep pens along the way. A cave was there and Saul went in to relieve himself and David and his men were far back in the cave. The men said, 'This is the day the Lord spoke of when He said, 'I will give your enemy into your hands for you to deal with as you wish." Then David crept up unnoticed and cut off a corner of Saul's robe. Afterwards David was conscious-stricken for having cut off a corner of his robe. He said to his men, 'The Lord forbid that I should do such a thing to my master, the Lord's anointed or lift up my hand against him for he is the anointed of the Lord.'"

Inspired by these words, the next week I went to see the head-teacher. She knew some Bible stories from childhood and of my faith. I told her about the story of David and Saul which I had heard the Sunday before. I said to her, "Be sure that I will never put a knife in your back by way of slanderous words about you in the staffroom or anywhere. Be assured of that. You have my full support. If on some point I disagree with you I will always tell you and you alone. I will not gossip about you to others behind your back." I felt her trust me and her gratitude from my words. I also noticed a tempering of the gossip in the staffroom, at least when I was present.

Many Christians today in schools, offices, or the workplace will have to live out their lives in a world of slanderous gossip and fight with the help of the Holy Spirit to be proved trustworthy.

Lesson 13

DECEPTION

KATIE WAS A VERY QUIET year 5 girl in one of my classes in 1991, always polite and respectful. She worked hard and didn't seem to get frustrated even though she struggled in some areas, including number skills. She sat next to a boy who was much better at maths. One day as the class were working quietly on number work I walked around checking how they were doing. As I looked over Katie's shoulder I could see she had surprisingly only two wrong answers. Looking at the boy beside her, he had made one uncharacteristic mistake and got a silly answer. When I looked back at Katie's work, one of her mistakes was the same as the boy's, the same silly answer.

"Katie, did you copy some of your answers of Paul, next to you?"

"No, sir," she replied.

I asked again and again she denied it, but her reddening face gave it away. I thought of Abraham's wife, Sarah, when she overheard the angels telling Abraham that Sarah would have a child. Sarah laughed to herself. She thought it impossible. When the angel confronted her, she denied it. So did Peter at the Lord's trial when challenged by a servant girl: "Surely you were with Him." He denied it. But I thought,

72   My Teaching Days

how many times have I lied rather than the truth be out, even as a Christian. Lying and deceitfulness are common in all walks of life. One teacher once asked why I did not apply for a higher position. "All you have to do at an interview is lie," she said. Lying begins at an early age and I found it commonplace among children. I found it necessary to call this sin though practice among most teachers was to call it "unacceptable" or "inappropriate behaviour." In Katie's case, she had broken two of the Lord's commandments—stolen an answer and lied about it. This was evil in His sight and I made that clear to children, always reminding them how I had been forgiven.

Lesson 14

CONFIDENCE IN APPROACHING GOD

THIS WAS A MESSAGE I prepared for a house group meeting in 1994, but the points mentioned were so very relevant to the situations I was going through in teaching and my personal life. I often needed supernatural help, and to have committed to memory Isaiah 41:10 so that many times I could shoot up a quick prayer and I received it straight away. Other promises eased fears, anxieties and worries immediately. "Cast all your cares on Him, for He cares for you," wrote Peter under the inspiration of the Holy Spirit.

In 1 John 5:14-15 the Apostle John makes a very bold statement by the inspiration of the Holy Spirit, which is worthy of much consideration. Verses 14 and 15 read, "This is the confidence we have in approaching God that if we ask anything according to His will, He hears us. And if we know that He hears us – whatever we ask – we know that we have what we asked of Him."

74   My Teaching Days

There are also two parallel verses elsewhere in Scripture which can confirm our understanding of 1 John 5:14-15. One is found earlier in 1 John 3:21-23:

> "Dear friends, if our hearts do not condemn us we have confidence before God and receive from Him anything we ask, because we obey His commands and do what pleases Him. And this is His command to believe in the name of His Son Jesus Christ and to love one another as He commanded us."

The other is found in Hebrews 10:19-23:

> "Therefore, brothers, since we have confidence to enter the Most Holy Place by the blood of Jesus by a new and living way opened up for us through the curtain that is His body, and since we have a great priest over the house of God, let us draw near in full assurance of faith having our hearts sprinkled to cleanse us from a guilty conscience and having our bodies washed with pure water. Let us hold unswervingly to the hope we profess, for He who promised is faithful."

These three passages tell all believers that they are to have confidence in approaching God. The Hebrew's verse uses the word "boldness" instead of "confidence." But what is the reason for this confidence, this boldness? It is not something we can conjure up from our own resources, in our own minds or by our own feelings. No, the preceding verses in 1 John 5 tell us in verse 11 that we have this confidence because He has given us eternal life and this life we have entered into is in His Son. We have entered into a living relationship with His Son and only those who have the Son have this life (1 John 5:12). It is a gift we could never earn, merit nor deserve. We simply received it by faith when He called us by His Spirit.

Confidence in Approaching God   75

Hebrews 10 enlarges this picture. We have confidence to come "by the blood of Jesus." He has opened a way through His death and resurrection "through the curtain that is His body." Moreover, He has now become a great priest over the house of God. We can come into the most Holy Place, where once only the high priest was allowed to go on behalf of the people because Jesus has opened the way. No longer does a curtain separate, we have confidence to come in.

1 John 3 says again that it is "because we have believed in the name of His Son," that we have confidence to approach our Heavenly Father. He also adds that we should guard our hearts, love one another and as Hebrews 10 reminds us, "have our hearts regularly sprinkled with the blood of the lamb to cleanse us from a guilty conscience" (Hebrews 10:22) so that "our hearts will not condemn us" (1 John 3:21).

So, we are to have confidence to approach God, completely by the merits of our Lord and Saviour, Jesus Christ alone, but then John makes this astounding statement in 1 John 5:14-15, "that if we ask anything according to his will, he hears us. And if we know that he hears us—whatever we ask—we know that we have what we asked of him." The key words here are "according to His will" and "we have what we asked of Him."

Some will say there are many areas where we do not know His will, and that is, of course, true. Within God's will there is both His revealed will as recorded in Scripture, but also there is His secret will which is not revealed. If we let our minds ignore what God has revealed, our confidence and boldness will be shaken and we can miss out. We should meditate on His revealed will, and boldly and confidently ask Him for clarification. The key, it seems to me, is rediscovering the lost discipline of learning more and more of God's

76   My Teaching Days

revealed will and memorising it so that the Spirit can bring it back to our mind. What a difference it would make to our confidence in approaching God with our requests and petitions.

So, may I suggest a few examples I have found helpful, where we can know God's revealed will and approach Him with confidence. I am sure there are many, many more you will call to mind.

Take "wisdom." "Heavenly wisdom" is needed every day. James 1:5 tells us "if any of you lack wisdom, he should ask God who gives generously without finding fault, so that you may be mature and complete, not lacking anything."

James 3:17-18 gives a picture of what true wisdom does not look like and what it does look like. James says that "the true wisdom that comes does from heaven is first of all pure; then peace-loving, considerate, submissive, full of mercy and good fruit, impartial and sincere. Peacemakers who sow in peace raise a harvest of righteousness."

The book of Proverbs also illustrates wisdom: " . . . for gaining wisdom and instruction; for understanding words of insight; for receiving instruction in prudent behaviour, doing what is right and just and fair; for giving prudence to those who are simple, knowledge and discretion to the young—let the wise listen and add to their learning (1:2-5). If we learn more of these wise words and we ask God for it, we know He gives it, we have it immediately and it becomes part of us.

Take our need for forgiveness. The promise is, "If we confess our sins He is faithful and just and will forgive our sins and cleanse us from all unrighteousness" (1 John 1:9). Our sins are remembered by Him no more and we should remember them no more. What a promise to immediately become ours! I am sure that when David asked

Confidence in Approaching God 77

God "to create a clean heart within him," he knew that he couldn't do it himself. He expected God to do it—but not the next year. He knew he had it even as he prayed.

Then there are situations where we are meeting difficulties, can't find something we need, can't cope. We become tense and fearful. We need help. And we can approach God confidently with just the simple plea "Help me!" because we know His will and His promise.

Isaiah 41:10 says, "So do not fear, for I am with you, do not be dismayed for I am your God. I will strengthen you and help you. I will uphold you with my righteous right hand."

Those words "Help me" may have been Nehemiah's quick prayer to God as he stood before King Cyrus. Many times did I, too, silently cry them out in my teaching days. I recall a time the class suddenly became noisy with chattering. Chaos was looming. I was ready to raise my voice disapprovingly, but before I did I shot up a quick "Help me" prayer to the King of Kings. Before I could raise my voice to the children, they all went quiet and got on with the work.

Or what about our need of a fresh filling of His Holy Spirit daily? In Luke 11:9-13 Jesus says, "So I say to you: Ask and it will be given to you; seek and you will find; knock and the door will be opened to you. For everyone who asks receives, he who seeks finds and to him who knocks the door will be opened. Which of you fathers, if your son asks for a fish will give him a snake instead. If you then, though you are evil, know how to give good gifts to your children, how much more will your father in Heaven give the Holy Spirit to those who ask Him!"

Note the tenses Jesus used. He is saying you can have this now. A fresh filling is available every day, as is the armour listed in Ephesians 6.

78   My Teaching Days

So many promises of God are revealed to us and are part of His revealed will for His followers here and now. They are available to all who come with a confident faith, because we know that we His beloved children.

But we can also have confidence to come before the throne of grace with matters we are ignorant of His will completely, confident in knowing that He hears us and that He cares because He says He does. We can come before God confident while also accepting there may not be a desired answer in the present here and now. The desired answer may come sometime in the future according to His perfect will and timing, or it may never come because in His sovereign omniscient will He knows best.

Into this area, come with prayers before the throne of grace for healing. We know that we can come confidently and that what we are requesting is not outside His will and purposes. The Lord Jesus was inundated by sick people when He walked the earth. He did not ignore them. Some men lowered a friend through the roof into a crowded room so we know we too can bring loved ones to Him with confidence knowing we will not be ignored and it is not outside His will to do so. We know from experience that we do not always get the reply we would like, but on many occasions, we do get the reply which we needed.

Another area where we are not promised an instant answer to our liking is the gift of children. Again, we can have confidence in praying, knowing that what we are asking is not outside His will. In Genesis, God told the first couple to be fruitful and to multiply. In Genesis 29:31 we read, "When the Lord saw that Leah was not loved, he opened her womb, but Rachel was barren." God's will and

Confidence in Approaching God 79

purpose is sovereign and we do not always know why. I have known Christian couples who have prayed and tried hard to have a child, but have remained childless. From my own experience, I recall pleading with God for Timothy and his wife, Hannah, for several years after their marriage. Patiently I waited for a positive answer knowing it might never come. On a visit to see them on a birthday, Timothy had planned a walk in the grounds of Chatsworth House in Derbyshire. As we walked the high hill overlooking the house, my son and his wife were some way ahead, walking hand in hand. My heart began to praise God for His wonderful creation and then to plead again that they would be blest with a child. As we caught up and drew near to them, Timothy turned and announced, "Dad, we have some good news for you and mum. There's going to be a new little Fairbrother in the family. Hannah's pregnant." In some amazement, belief mingled with unbelief, I thanked my Heavenly Father.

It is a similar situation when we plead with God to reveal His salvation to loved ones, family members who know Him not. We do not know fully His omniscient sovereign will. Jonah declared, "Salvation is of the Lord." The prophet Isaiah declared, "His arm is not too short to save." But He is sovereign in His choosing of souls. Jesus said, "No one comes to me unless the Father draws them," and the miracle is that He chooses anybody. No one deserves it. It is a miracle that He chose me. We cannot dictate to Him whom He should save, but it is with confidence that we can plead knowing that salvation is within His will while accepting that He is sovereign regarding whom He chooses.

I prayed for my own children from the moment they were conceived. God called one when he was 16 years old, the other when he was 19 years old. I never say that God saved them because of my earnest pleading. Ephesians 2 says He saves people "according to His own good will and pleasure." I would never say to young parents with children, "pray earnestly every day and He will definitely save them eventually," because He may not. I urge them to pray, such is the mystery of not knowing His secret will, but with the knowledge that their requests may not be granted.

These two sides of God's will are always at work. Our duty is to desire to know His will more and more so that we will have confidence in approaching God.

Lesson 15

COMPLETE IN JESUS

AROUND THE YEAR 2000, TIMOTHY gave me a book for Christmas titled "Look No Hands." It was the autobiography of a Northern Ireland man, Brian Gault, who was born without arms as a result of his mother taking the drug thalidomide in the early 1960s while pregnant. Brian had been speaking at our son's church in Sheffield and Timothy bought the book at the end, signed by Brian with his toes. Having read the book, including Brian's dramatic conversion to Christ, I contacted him through email since the address was listed at the end of the book. While reading, I learned that Brian had told his story at events all over the world, so I asked if he had ever been to the big city of Birmingham. And so began a series of visits over a period of four years. I had many contacts in schools and all were eager to have a visit from Brian. If I had said would they like a visit from a Christian evangelist, most would have been unsure. Instead, I introduced him as a man who had overcome many obstacles in his life, though I had to be honest and say he would include a few words about how he became a Christian, too.

Brian delighted the children from as young as five years old to age seventeen. He showed them how he could take the wrapper off a chocolate bar with his toes, then invited some children to take off their shoes and socks

Brian Gault with no arms in a Primary classroom taking the cover off a chocolate bar with his toes.

and have a go. In one school, he played table tennis with a boy. He held the bat between his chin and shoulder and could maneuverer it very well. The children were amazed. Then he would tell them how, as a boy, he was very angry with God for making him armless but said how a boy with down syndrome shared with him at special school how much Jesus loved him by dying on a cross for him to forgive him. Now he could say that God didn't make any mistakes when He formed him in his mother's womb. "Now I'm complete in Jesus," he would say.

We also took Brian into prisons, a night shelter for homeless men, senior citizens clubs as well as many churches. Some of the homeless people cried when they heard Brian's story. Sadly, as Brian made us aware, thalidomide was still being given to pregnant women for morning sickness in countries in South America and even in 2004, children were born without limbs. Every term leading up to Easter, the staff encouraged the children to think of ingenious ideas to raise money for a cause. One idea I witnessed while doing supply work was to serve lunch to children on special tables at dinner time. The children serving wore waiter or waitresses' clothes and served extras to the ordinary school dinner such as special drinks and choice of sweets. They had a waiting list of children willing to pay for the service. That year, after Brian's visit, the cause chosen was a little girl Brian knew of who badly needed a special wheelchair to be able to go to school. The wheelchair would cost over £3,000 but the children worked hard in lunchtimes with ingenious ideas. Parents gave and over £4,000 was raised for the little girl born with no legs. God certainly used Brian to reach many children's hearts.

Lesson 16

ARROW PRAYERS

WHEN I LEFT FULL-TIME TEACHING, I did some supply teaching in different parts of the city around 2001. I chose to go into difficult areas—one area was an inner-city Church of England school with a very multi-racial intake. On my first morning, I called the register in a Year 6 class. Their names astounded me. Many had Old Testament names like Ezekiel or Obadiah. I commented on this and asked if they knew that these names were Old Testament names.

One boy from the back shouted out, "Are you a Bible basher, sir?" A Bible basher was one who consistently forces Scripture on others. He proved to be quite difficult before the first playtime and I told him to go and see the headteacher with a note. After 15 minutes, he had not returned. The bell went for play and I went to see the headteacher. She said she had not seen him. She told me he frequently ran out of school, and I did not see him for the rest of the day.

I decided to go back if asked, and my next visit was for an afternoon. The teacher asked me if I would teach two different classes the Ten Commandments. The first class of younger children listened and wrote about them well. But the second class of older children were very different. I was shooting up arrow prayers, like Nehemiah must have been doing as cupbearer before King Cyrus when he was asked why he looked so sad. As I mentioned the Bible, there was noise. The noise only went down a little as I read the first commandments. When I got to "do not commit adultery," I thought I should explain what "adultery" meant and point out what Jesus said about looking at a woman with lust in your heart. I then said, amid some noise, that I would tell them a story from the New Testament about Jesus meeting a woman caught in adultery by some religious leaders who were about to stone her to death. At this point, a big boy sitting at the front stood up, turned to the class and said, "Shut up all of you, we want to hear this!" The room became silent and I read the story. There were some mouths open when I told them the words Jesus spoke to the leaders: "Let him who is without sin throw the first stone." There was complete silence from then on. God heard Nehemiah's prayer and He heard mine. The shortest arrow prayer "help me, help," is never in vain.

God has promised us in Isaiah 41:10: "So do not fear . . . I will strengthen you and help you . . . "

Lesson 17

OPENING DOORS

AFTER RETIRING FROM FULL-TIME TEACHING in the late 1990s, I found some regular contract work in a school on a council estate on the outer parts of the city. Many of the children were from broken families and this was a new experience for me. The children had little or no knowledge of the Bible. Even though I was getting older, I still loved playing outside games with children and teaching good sporting skills. I discovered that the school never had a football team, but there were several boys who liked playing. At that time, we had a Brazilian family working with our church, and even though Jose was into his thirties he was a skilled footballer. He offered to come and help me train the boys once a week after school. I cleared all this with the headteacher and before training Jose gave a short talk on why Jesus had come into the world. He offered them a simple tract around the subject of football and all the boys accepted this and took them home. This activity opened doors for me at lunchtime when I used to sit with the children. Many of the 11-year-old boys came to my dinner table to ask questions about Jesus.

86   My Teaching Days

Then another door was opened when the deputy head asked me if I would like to do an assembly on Abraham sacrificing his son. I willingly accepted and on the day, I dramatised the story with myself as Abraham and a child as Isaac. At the end, I pointed out how God provided the sacrifice looking ahead to when He would provide the ultimate sacrifice for sin by giving His own son to the world. I finished by quoting John 3:16. Staff present were moved and some thanked me for making it so real. The footballing boys asked more questions at dinner that day.

On another occasion, towards Christmas I had to tell the Christmas story. I explained that the name Joseph was told to give his son was "Jesus," meaning "Saviour." I told them that He saved people from the punishment they deserved for their wrongdoing by taking the punishment Himself when He gave His life on the cross. I said I was grateful He took my punishment. When I had finished one boy at the back of the class confessed quite loudly, "I think I need a saviour."

The head and deputy suddenly became unhappy about the training we were doing, possibly because of the talks my friend was doing or the tracts we passed out, so my contract ended. But I felt God was closing one door and that He would open more. He did.

That was my prayer wherever I was asked to go, that God would open doors. My prayers were based on God's word to Abraham in Genesis 12:2: "I will make you into a great nation and I will bless you I will make your name great and you will be a blessing."

So I prayed: "Bless me Lord, make me a blessing to these children. Do me good and help me to do them good."

In one school I went to, I arrived to hear that the teacher whose class I would be taking had removed a 10-year-old girl whom he

Opening Doors   87

thought would give me great difficulties. I had a good day with the children, encouraging them not to give up if they found something difficult. Helping them improve their skills in drawing, painting, writing, mental arithmetic and a chance to do some ball skills with a game to finish. They really enjoyed this. At the end of the day the excluded girl came in just as the children were leaving. They were telling her what we had done. They all left except the girl. She came up to my desk. I had an open Bible on it which I had been just about to read. She asked what I had done with the children and seemed sorry she had missed it. Then she asked, "What's that you're reading, sir?" The passage was 1 John 1, so I read the verses 5-10 so she could follow. I explained what sin was in terms of some sins which she—and indeed all children—commit. I said that I committed sins as well, but stressed how the passage tells us that God forgives and remembers no more, for "the blood of His son purifies from all sin." She listened carefully, said "thank you," and left pondering. Where, I wonder, is she now? Did God move by His Spirit in her life?

On another occasion in a Church of England school, with a Year 6 class of very intelligent children, I was asked by the teacher to do a religious education (RE) lesson about Red Nose Day, which was coming up. Red Nose Day is an annual fundraising campaign with the goal to end poverty. It is sponsored by the non-profit organization Comic Relief, Inc. in the U.K. and the United States. The teacher told me we were raising money for the local hospital. This is about giving, I thought. There was a Bible in the classroom, so with the children sitting around me, I read some Scripture to them. Jesus taught in Matthew 6 about giving in secret from "the widow who gave all she

88 My Teaching Days

had." Do not let your left hand know what your right hand is doing. The children were stunned. We went on with the other lessons of the day, and as they left, a Muslim boy came to me and said, "Thank you for that teaching about giving, I've never heard anything like that before." Has he read more in a Bible somewhere since then?

One time I was told I could do anything I wanted to in an RE lesson, so I decided grace was the subject. I started by playing a recording of George Beverley Shea singing "Amazing Grace," then asked them to look at Ephesians 2 in the Bibles the school had. While the children were writing about what they had learned about grace, I walked around the room. Two twin sisters got my attention. They were children of an Anglican vicar. They were musing over their Bible, so I sat with them and turned to Romans 3. We read the words together, "no one is righteous, no not one, no one who does good," and, "If God alone is righteous, then how, I asked could anyone come before Him." Then we read on, "But now a righteousness from God has been revealed . . . " It was a joy to talk with those twins, and again, I sometimes ponder has God's Spirit been working in them since.

In another infant school I enjoyed going to in the early 2000s, I had to lead the class I was taking into the hall for what was termed as singing practice. As I seated the children in position, an older lady pianist was playing "Be Still for the Presence of the Lord." I went across to her and complimented her for what she was playing.

"Yes," she said, "but this local authority is trying to de-Christianize all sectors of education."

Yes, I thought, multi-faith is the order of the day.

It has been a joy to sow seed, a joy to tell children they are made in the image of God, and are fearfully and wonderfully made and not a product of evolution. I told the children when they seemed a little convicted about sin that I was much worse than them as a child. They would ask me what sort of things I used to do wrong as a child. There were too many to tell them, all I could say was that I have been forgiven of every one. Jesus' blood has wiped out all. God remembers them no more and neither do I. Nor did I pretend that I was already perfect, I still did wrong sometimes unwittingly and deliberately. But as I would tell the children I can always admit it to God and know that Jesus' blood shed 2,000 years ago can still wipe out every one.

Isaiah 1:18 says, "Come now, let us settle the matter, says the Lord. Though your sins are like scarlet, they shall be as white as snow."

What a joy to share Scripture in handwriting lessons! A favourite of mine when I was asked to do handwriting on supply was to write neatly on the board, a line at a time the verses from 1 Corinthians 13 about love.

Or what of the Muslim girl who came to my classroom one lunchtime when I was alone eating my sandwiches.

"Do you believe Jesus is God, sir?"

"Yes Misba I do," I said.

This same girl took part in a class assembly I did. I chose four proverbs from the Bible and asked the children to devise a sketch to illustrate a proverb. This they did very well.

Over a year later, Misba came to me while I was on playground duty and said, "I still remember that proverb we did," and she recited it to me. The word of God is living and active. Might she have come across some Christians at university who talked with her more? God is sovereign in whom He chooses as Christians and He alone knows.

90 My Teaching Days

I have learned that children like structure and order, they like encouragement, fairness and just discipline, they liked to be loved. When I was teaching full time one Muslim boy came to me once and asked, "Why do you keep on teaching us good things when a lot of the children treat you so badly?" What I hope he was asking was, "Why do you keep on loving us?" because that is what I was commanded to do. Jesus said, "Love your enemies, pray for those who persecute you." Most children respect honesty but only Jesus can give them truth.

I have tried to teach children to see God in everything. In science lessons, I pointed out that every theory was devised by God—friction, solubility, and atomic physics. Men only discovered the theories. When teaching primary children about electricity, I loved to give a history lesson on Michael Faraday and his faith. God is in all history for it is His story. He devised numbers, all nature, languages, music— He is the perfect designer.

Lesson 18

WITNESSING TO FELLOW TEACHERS

I WAS CHALLENGED IN MY early days as a Christian by Paul's request to the Colossian church in Colossians 4:2-4: "Devote yourselves to prayer, being watchful and thankful. And pray for us, too, that God may open a door for our message so that we may proclaim the mystery of Christ, for which I am in chains. Pray that I may proclaim it clearly, as I should."

I began to pray this prayer for myself whenever I went into different schools and indeed, wherever I went. It was no surprise, then, that doors did open. Like Paul, I felt that God meant business when He opened doors. Similar to Paul's sentiment in 2 Corinthians 5, I became conscious that we were co-workers with Him in the ministry of reconciliation. In some schools I went to on supply, doors opened in staff rooms and with teachers in their classrooms at the end of the day. Sometimes a door was opened for the message and I was not ready. Then I remembered Peter's word in his letter in 1 Peter 3:15: "But in your hearts set apart Christ as Lord. Always be prepared to give an

92   My Teaching Days

answer to everyone who asks you to give the reason for the hope you have. But do this with gentleness and respect."

But many times, I was able to have a good but short conversation about the Lord with a staff member. The outcomes were varied and this caused me to ponder. In some cases, the message seemed to be well received and I was welcomed back for more work in the school. However, in other cases, though the conversations seemed cordial, I later sensed an air of opposition and no further work was offered in that school, even though I felt a genuine door had been opened with the staff member asking me questions . . . I pondered on this and how it was in the days when the Lord Jesus walked the earth and in the early church just after His ascension. Doors opened as He spoke to crowds of Jews, Jewish leaders, Pharisees and teachers. They asked questions of Him and some received the message gladly. Others seemed to listen, then quietly walked away. But then, perhaps conversing with others they turned nasty, they took Him, beat Him, gave Him a false trial, and crucified Him, for they did not understand Isaiah's prophesy in Isaiah 53:10: "Yet it was the Lord's will to crush him." "But it was not the end of the story for many who heard Him speak and then turned away. As the early church grew in numbers, as recorded in Acts 6:7, we read: "So the word of God spread. The number of disciples in Jerusalem increased rapidly, and a large number of priests became obedient to the faith."

Although on a less grander level, the slights I felt from the schools had been felt before by my Saviour. As I pondered all these things and related them to the fact that although I did not get a further request for work, someone may have listened well to my

Witnessing to Fellow Teachers   93

presentation of the Lord. Did He use that seed that had been sown, make it grow and come alive? And if He did, are they now serving the Lord in some church somewhere? It always was, and still is comforting to know that He always has been and always will be the Lord of the harvest. Sowing seed is never in vain, even when there seems to be no immediate result or conversion. It has been a joy to be the Lord's servant, sowing seed in so many different schools, trusting Him completely according to His own good will and pleasure.

Prayer is so vital, it is the Christian's native air. The Lord Jesus urged His people never to give up praying and being thankful. He said, "ask, and you will receive." I found this to be true when I was seeking supply work, having come out of full time teaching in my fifties. I was conscious that I still had the responsibility of providing for my family. My children were going through university and I could not fail them. I can testify that I maintained my quiet time with God early in the morning, put on the spiritual armour. I found it amazing—knowing that I needed work—when I was on my knees in prayer, I would get to a petition that the Lord would meet my daily needs, my daily bread and help me to earn that daily bread. At that point in the prayer I was completely amazed that so many times the telephone would ring with a request to go to a school I actually liked going to. He knows what we need before we ask Him.

There is another verse on prayer I learned a long time ago—it comes in 1 John 5:14-15: "This is the confidence we have in approaching God: that if we ask anything according to his will, he hears us. And if we know that he hears us—whatever we ask—we know that

94   My Teaching Days

we have what we asked of him." I felt it was His will that a man should earn the food that he eats, that he should not be lazy but work, and so I had what I asked Him not a week later, or a month later, but immediately. What a generous God.

Lesson 19

THE SINAI DESERT

IN 2006, A POSTER APPEARED on the church notice board about a walk in the Sinai Desert, organized by the Edinburgh Medical Mission, to raise funds for a hospital in Malawi. My only previous flight had been from Birmingham airport to the Isle of Man, about half an hour. I was excited by the challenge. I thought of saints of old like Abraham, Joshua or Moses who were faced with exciting challenges, new experiences not done before, not sure what lay ahead, and how they stepped out in faith. I applied and was accepted and went out into the unknown with a group of other Christians who encouraged and helped me.

When I returned, I thought of schools I knew of through some friends, and I was welcomed to share some lessons learned from my adventures which would apply to young children. The first lesson was from the staggering creation—I showed some pictures from my travels. Was it all created by God, or did it just appear by chance? I told them I believed God created it and read a few words from Genesis 1, and I praised Him every day I was there.

96 My Teaching Days

Then, there was the lesson about facing challenges. I took as an example an Old Testament saint like Moses leading the people out of Egypt, Joshua leading the people of Israel into the promised land or David facing Goliath. All the children knew the promise of God not to be afraid, for He had said, "I am with you wherever you go." I reminded the children that they had already faced many challenges like going to playgroup, infant, junior school for the first time.

Then, closely linked to facing challenges was the thought of not giving up. In the hot burning desert, that thought came across some minds when the walking got tough. There were some steep climbs up and some awesome climbs down. One or two of the older walkers elected to take a camel sometimes and go a longer way around. I showed some pictures of the difficult drops and said it would have been easy to say, "I can't do this bit." Lots of children I have taught over the years have said to me, "I can't do it," or, "I don't know how to do this." So, I reminded the children of how they learned to walk by progressing through each stage. I crawled along the floor and reminded them that this was how they moved about for weeks. Then I pulled myself up, holding on to a table, but would not let go, inching my way along the table then one step holding on to nothing as I reached out for the next piece of furniture. This, too, I reminded them they would do for weeks. A tough job learning to walk. But, I told them, if at any stage they decided to give up, then they would still be crawling to school at age ten. All skills, I told them, take time to learn—swimming, horse riding, playing a musical instrument, even learning to spell, but if the mindset is "I can't do this," then they would never do it. Nearly all of us got up the steep climbs and down the dangerous drops safely. We had expert Arab guides.

On Mount Sinai 2006.

I learned another lesson in the desert—to always follow good advice or rules. I told them God has given us good rules to live by and I asked the children if they knew any of the Ten Commandments. I told them I had to learn a painful lesson walking in the desert. We were sent lots of papers before the trip to help us prepare. One good piece of advice given was to take a pair of sunglasses. I ignored this, thinking I'd never worn sunglasses while walking hills in a warm, sunny English summer. But a day after walking the desert, my eyes began to weep and run. I had to keep rubbing them. Here was the reflection from the hot, dry white sand not found on the hills of England. Fortunately, we had a doctor accompanying us, carrying various medicines and creams and he applied some to my eyes. A fellow Christian walker had a spare pair of sunglasses which he let me have. How important to obey good advice and rules. I told the children that the Bible says that children should obey their parents and their teachers.

Lesson 20

COMPETING IDEAS AND PHILOSOPHIES

WHEN I WAS TRAINING TO be a teacher we studied different philosopher's writings on education, people like Piaget and the Frenchman Jean Jacques Rousseau. The latter expressed his views in a book called "Emile." Basically, Emile was born good and needed good materials, a good working environment, good stimuli, good teaching and he would turn out an excellent pupil. He didn't blame Emile, he blamed the educators. As I grew in my Christian faith I learned that a child is as David described himself in Psalm 51: "Surely I was sinful at birth, sinful from the time my mother conceived me." Not born good as Rousseau thought every child was. Sadly in my days of teaching many parents thought the same about their children, and even more sad some teachers and headteachers thought the same. The view taken was that evil behaviour was to be called unacceptable behaviour and children should be offered good incentives not to do it again, such as a free trip to a McDonald's restaurant.

One day I kept a boy in at lunchtime to do some extra work. He had been rude and lazy. I let him go when it was time for his lunch.

100   My Teaching Days

The head caught him going down the stairs and asked him what he was doing inside school. After lunch, I was standing at the front explaining some work to the listening children when the head burst in. He stopped me teaching and asked why I had kept that boy in at lunchtime. What had he done wrong to warrant my action? I protested and said I would see him at the end of the day but he persisted. He was not happy that the child's behaviour warranted the punishment. He did not support me, but rather thought the child had a case. Surely, I thought this Headteacher does not believe as David does in Psalm 51, but leans to the views of Rousseau. The two views are diametrically opposed. If David is right then there is a desperate need of a Saviour. If Rousseau is right man is master of his own fate and never wrong.

When after retirement I moved into supply teaching, I began to meet children who were given the drug Ritalin for attention deficit disorder (ADD), or attention deficit hyperactivity disorder (ADHD). I was given a paper by a Christian friend, a doctor, explaining some of the dangers of this drug. The paper had been written by a Christian medic and warned that it could lead the child to take even harder drugs in later life.

I remember taking one class and being warned by the teacher upon my arrival that there was a boy who could be hyperactive and would need a tablet at 11:30 a.m. He started to be a bit loud and the child next to him said, "He's hyperactive, he'll need a tablet in a bit." I thought I would tackle the problem differently. I went up to the boy, stood above him (I'm quite tall) and with a big, stern voice said, "You are rude, loud and lazy and not working as God intends." There was silence and the boy put his head down and started to work.

11:30 a.m. came, then 12:00 p.m. and he was still working. The bell went for lunch time and I said, "You haven't had your tablet yet."

"Oh," he said, and went straight out to play without taking the tablet.

On another occasion, the teacher asked me to do a lesson on the Greeks. There was a timeline on the wall with the letters B.C. and A.D. She asked me to refer to this and talk about the B.C. and A.D. This I did with a sense of meaning in my voice. One boy quizzed me about Christ and I gave a succinct reply which conveyed that I believed and got on with the Greek lesson. That evening I had a call from the local authority head of supply teaching with the message: you may not speak about God in any more schools. A parent it seemed had been to the school to complain. God has always been building His kingdom, I thought, and the kingdoms of the world have always been in opposition.

Lesson 21

MEETING CHALLENGING BEHAVIOUR

I REMEMBER THE WEEK MY teacher union announced a survey was completed among a large sample of teachers. They found that four out of ten teachers were attacked in the classroom in 2015 and that children's behaviour was worsening. It seems to me that there is a war going on in the field of education, a war that has been going on since the late 1980s as different philosophies and opinions for dealing with difficult children with evil, violent behaviour were argued about. In the meantime, we have witnessed such many teachers injured in attacks, as well as other pupils.

One viewpoint I've come across is children should not be punished as it may not be completely their fault. The teacher may share the greater blame because of bad management of the class or not enough planning went into making the lesson interesting. Punishing children, they argue, produces even worse behaviour. Another line taken is that instead of punishing, it is better to offer rewards if the

104   My Teaching Days

child tries to be good for a week, a reward such as a trip to a bowling alley. Some professionals recognise that this is not fully effective because as soon as the rewards stop, a child goes back to his or her bad ways. When I read about these efforts to get children to be good, it reminded me of a class I once had with some very difficult children while supply teaching. At the end of the day, two lovely girls, who had been no trouble at all, came to me and said, "We've been good today, haven't we sir? Can we have some house points?" My reply was, "Well that is what you should be. You should be good every day, without any reward. The Lord God wants you to be good." It was a Church of England school and they did hear some good messages in assembly so I felt it right to bring God into the picture.

So why do all these different philosophies and ideas miss the mark? It is simply because God and His word are left out of the picture. The truth is that children have always exhibited evil behaviour since the days of Adam and Eve. Adam's sin imputed to every conceived child. Each child must be responsible for his or her own words or deeds, not blaming anyone else, not blaming another child or a teacher. Indeed, every teacher must be responsible before God for his or her own thoughts, words and deeds.

Jesus did not come into the world to say that sin does not matter or that there will be no punishment. He did not proclaim, "punishment will do you no good, let me tell you what rewards you will receive if only you try very hard to be good. You will like these rewards."

No, in God's eyes, sin does matter and must be punished. For all of us it goes back to the time we were conceived and in the mother's womb, even sinful there. That is why Jesus came, for no other reason but to take the punishment for all those many, many sins that they

Meeting Challenging Behaviour 105

may be wiped from our record and to give us the Holy Spirit to work the good in us which we could never work ourselves. I know of quite many people who accepted the call of Jesus while young and still at school. They testify of the power of the cross and the power of the Holy Spirit leading them in righteous paths. No philosophy of man, no matter how well thought out, no matter how persuasively delivered can change the heart of a Cain, a Jezebel, or any human heart. Jeremiah 17:9 says, "the human heart is deceitful above all things and beyond cure."

After I became a Christian I had a new perspective on so many areas of life. In the mid-1970s it was still permissible in schools to use corporal punishment if children were woefully disobedient. This I had done before I was a Christian, but as a believer I never administered any punishment in anger or frustration. I knew the instructions for fathers in the book of Ephesians, "fathers do not exasperate your children," and I had my own children by then. I believed that they could become exasperated if they saw me uncontrolled or unfair when I was disciplining them. So, I felt any punishment should be just, contained and immediate. I felt the last point very important so that I could say, once administered, "That's over now, put it behind us and let's enjoy the games lesson this afternoon." I loved joining in with them in games activities.

In 1984, however, there was a huge debate to remove all corporal punishment from schools. There was a joint union vote in the staffroom on the matter, and I was the only member to vote in favour of keeping it. For that I was ridiculed and abuse was hurled at me, but I stood by what I believed and would vote the same way today. The Secretary of State for Education at the time, Keith Joseph, I felt dealt with the matter in a weak way, and parliament voted to abolish corporal punishment in schools.

The immediate impact once the decision had been taken caused even worse behaviour. Rude children now felt unstoppable to shout into my face, "You can't touch me now. I can do what I like." They were very difficult days, but I determined that such rude, defiant behaviour should not be ignored but met with strength and boldness coming from the Lord. I had always encouraged children struggling with work not to give up, and I was not going to give up now in controlling children.

I knew well the verses in Hebrews 12:8-11 on God's discipline on His children:

> "If you are not disciplined—and everyone undergoes discipline—then you are not legitimate, not true sons and daughters at all. Moreover, we have all had human fathers who disciplined us and we respected them for it. How much more should we submit to the Father of spirits and live! They disciplined us for a little while as they thought best; but God disciplines us for our good, in order that we may share in his holiness. No discipline seems pleasant at the time, but painful. Later on, however, it produces a harvest of righteousness and peace for those who have been trained by it."

I was saddened by the reactions of members of staff who had voted for the abolition. Frequently I could hear teachers in adjoining classrooms frantically shouting at children with inappropriate threats. One day I was on playground duty with the deputy head and was standing near him. I had once known him as a strong disciplinarian whom the children feared. A child came up to him crying

Meeting Challenging Behaviour   107

and asking for help because he was being bullied and threatened by a bigger, older boy who was standing close by ready to argue with the deputy. The deputy didn't even look at the crying child. "Oh, go away," he said, and I saw he felt powerless. But I resolved that I would not throw in the towel, that I would meet bad, rude and troublesome behaviour in the playground or in the classroom with power and strength from the Lord. I remembered Joshua who heard the Lord's voice in Joshua 1:6,9: "Be strong and courageous . . . do not be terrified, do not be discouraged for the Lord your God will be with you wherever you go." There was David who did not back down and run away from the problem. He said to the Philistine Goliath, twice his size, "You come against me with sword and spear but I come against you in the name of the Lord Almighty, the God of Israel." I knew of Moses as the people came to the Red Sea. They were ready to give in and grumbled to Moses. Exodus 14:13-14 says, "Moses answered the people, 'Do not be afraid. Stand firm and you will see the deliverance the Lord will bring you today. The Egyptians you see today you will never see again. The Lord will fight for you; you need only to be still." What a promise as true today as it was then.

So, I met rude comments with a strong voice as I stood upright before them: "That was rude and bad mannered, it was evil and came from your evil heart." They shuddered at the word "evil" but that is what Jesus would have called it. They did not like being thought of as evil. I gave a strict warning that if they repeated it they would stay in and do extra work at playtime and dinnertime. My only regret was that the punishment could not be immediate. Gradually, though, they came to know that I was a man who kept my word, I did not change my mind. I did not issue a punishment out of frustration and

108 My Teaching Days

I was fair. They were, after all, children and I was the adult with authority. I introduced order and structure at the beginning of the day. Mine was the only class which had to line up quietly outside the classroom before being told to enter. This I had to enforce at first as they saw other children in other classes alongside entering noisily and somewhat wildly. Once in, they stood behind their chairs till they were told to sit. In time, they liked the order and structure of it. Some children were always quiet and wanted to work hard and I felt I had to protect them from those children who liked to bring chaos to the room. I marked their work carefully and gave them a score so they could evaluate how well they were doing and so they could see improvement.

Here I must confess that before I became a Christian, I sometimes would not even read some pupil's work but just tick and put a comment which wasn't much help. They loved the scores and as the first term went on after corporal punishment was abolished I never heard rude comments called out. I tried to love them as I did my own children and what I wanted for my own children, I wanted for them. As I considered this issue of "challenging behaviour," I thought about my own childhood at school. Three times my behaviour warranted a caning, which looking back I can say I fully deserved, as I have deserved God's discipline. I thought also of the area where I lived then. There was there a very old 17th century schoolhouse on the green. On occasions, you could go inside with a curator and see old documents like the one charting the injuries, the broken bones suffered by the teacher who was also the local rector as he wrestled with unruly students in the 17th century. Times change. Our God is unchanging, still all powerful. Children cannot be allowed to do what they like.

I was working hard with my own children, teaching them the Lord's commands and all the Holy Scriptures, making them wise unto salvation. My wife and I have had the joy of seeing the Lord speak to both Timothy and Andrew. We have heard their great confession of faith, seen them go through the waters of baptism, and more importantly seen them continue in Him in Christian service. God has given them Christian wives and they now have their own children to bring up. My prayer each day is that they too will see the salvation of their children in their lifetime, as we have done. It must be the prayer of many Christian parents, and there must be many Christian teachers still facing difficult, disruptive pupils as I did way back in the 1980s.

For more information about

John Fairbrother

and

My Teaching Days
please contact:

thefairbrothers@googlemail.com

For more information about
AMBASSADOR INTERNATIONAL
please visit:

www.ambassador-international.com
@AmbassadorIntl
www.facebook.com/AmbassadorIntl

Printed in Poland
by Amazon Fulfillment
Poland Sp. z o.o., Wrocław